Grandpa's

Furry and Feathered

Friends

Other books by Jan Doward

Even the Angels Must Laugh Again
Finding The Right Path
When All Alone I Stand (R&H)

Grandpa's
Furry and Feathered
Friends

Meet Stubbytail, Hop-Hops, and all the other
birds and animals at Grandpa's place

JAN S. DOWARD

Pacific Press® Publishing Association
Nampa, Idaho
Oshawa, Ontario, Canada
www.pacificpress.com

Designed by Dennis Ferree
Cover illustration by Carol Strebel
Inside photos by Jan S. Doward

Additional copies of this book are available by
calling toll free 1-800-765-6955 or visiting
http://www.adventistbookcenter.com

Library of Congress Cataloging-in-Publication data:

Doward, Jan S.
Grandpa's furry and feathered friends:meet Stubbytail,
Hop-Hops, and all other birds and animals at Grandpa's
place/Jan S. Doward.
p. cm.
Summary: Grandpa shares stories about chipmunks,
humming birds, wood rats, deer, and other birds and animals
that live around his house.
ISBN: 0-8163-1952-9
1. Animals—Juvenile. [1. Animals.] I. Title.
PZ10.3.D7268 Gr 2003
—dc21   2002035549

03 04 05 06 07 • 5 4 3 2 1

Dedication

To my grandchildren:
Erin,
Kailey,
Tait,
Trent,
&
Dallas

Contents

Surprises in the Birdhouses

Just as Grandpa stepped off the back porch, he heard a high-pitched sound.

"Chip! Chip! Chip!"

"Now what kind of bird makes a call like that?" he wondered.

Many different birds come to Grandpa's place and they sing all sorts of sweet songs. Others like the woodpecker make a tap, tap, tapping sound as they bore into a tree. But what kind of bird would make a chipping sound?

There it was again just as loud as before.

"Chip! Chip! Chip!"

Grandpa turned his head to follow the sound. Just across the driveway, he spotted a chipmunk sitting on top of the woodpile. As he watched, it said, *"Chip! Chip! Chip!"* and its tail jerked up and down with each sound.

"Well, well," Grandpa said with a smile, "it isn't a bird after all." Slowly he walked toward the woodpile trying not to scare the cute little creature.

"Chip! Chip! Chip!" came the call again.

Bending closer toward the woodpile, Grandpa looked right into the chipmunk's face. "Now what are you saying?" he asked.

The only answer from the chipmunk was more, *"Chip! Chip! Chip!"*

But from that moment on, Grandpa could always tell the chipmunk's call. No bird around his place sounds quite like this tiny striped animal.

One day Grandpa happened to be looking toward the big spruce tree on the west side of his driveway and he saw something strange. In the red birdhouse on a pole, not far from the tree, he thought he saw something moving. It was not the time of the year for the birds to be nesting. What could it be? Suddenly two baby chipmunks stuck their heads out of the birdhouse hole.

"Well, well," Grandpa said with a smile, "so this is where you've been living."

The baby chipmunks did not answer, but one of them was brave enough to creep out onto the tiny perch on the front of the birdhouse. The other one stayed behind watching very closely. After all, it was a long way down to the ground.

"Now you be careful," Grandpa warned.

The brave baby chipmunk wanted to go exploring but he got scared too. He started to back up. But just then, his brother moved a little farther out of the birdhouse hole so he could see more. With a tiny thump, he bumped into his brave brother. And that's when it happened! The brave little chipmunk fell! It was a long, long way to the ground, but the brave little chipmunk spread his legs out like wings and sailed right down. He landed on the soft spruce needles on the ground and it didn't hurt a bit. After a moment, he scampered away.

Grandpa took the picture, he talked to the baby chipmunk.

"You don't seem ready to follow your brother, do you?"

No, indeed. Baby chipmunk ducked back inside and stayed out of sight until he felt a lot braver. Grandpa was sure that when the brave brother climbed back up the pole to the birdhouse, he would have all sorts of stories to tell about his big adventure into the woods around Grandpa's place.

Every year before the tree swallows return, Grandpa puts on his work gloves, climbs up a ladder and cleans out the old bird nests from the birdhouses. But now that he knew that chipmunks were raising families in the birdhouses, too, he would have to check for them before he cleaned out the old nests.

One day, he took the roof off the white birdhouse on the big tree in his backyard. Inside was something strange. What was it? No chipmunks were inside, but neither was there a bird's nest. It was a big ball of soft, fluffy, moss, shredded bark, and dried grass all ready for a chipmunk family. Mama chipmunk wanted to make sure she had a nice place for her babies. Very gently, Grandpa lifted the soft ball. His eyes widened as he stared at the bottom of the birdhouse.

"Well, look at that!" he exclaimed. Right there on the left side of the birdhouse floor was a whole row of neatly stacked birdseed. Amazingly, the grain had all been sorted out. There was wheat, millet, milo, and sunflower seeds all in separate piles stored away for the chipmunk family.

Grandpa didn't know what to do. "The chipmunk wants this spot for her family. But the swallows will be coming soon and they'll want their house back."

Then an idea came to him. Several years before, a rancher had given Grandpa some nice little wooden boxes, "coyote boxes," and one of these would make an ideal chipmunk house. He could transfer everything from the birdhouse and then both the chipmunks and birds would be happy. Grandpa smiled to himself. "I'll just use one of those 'coyote boxes!' "

What is a "coyote box," you ask? It all started when this rancher friend tried an experiment to chase the coyotes away from his sheep. He had built the boxes to hold a loud speaker, a tape recorder, and some batteries. The idea was to play a recording of dogs barking whenever coyotes came near the sheep. The moment the coyotes heard the barking, they would run away for sure. The coyote boxes worked fine the first year. But after that, the great invention failed. Why? Because after that, Mama and Papa coyote taught their young that no dogs were really around. They had learned that the barking wasn't real. This was why the rancher gave Grandpa all of his "coyote boxes" to use as birdhouses.

Grandpa did turn some of the coyote boxes into birdhouses, but now he picked one to turn into a chipmunk house. Very carefully, he scooped up all of the little piles of grain and placed them on the floor of the coyote box exactly like it had been in the birdhouse. Then he put the soft moss and dried grass on top just like Mama chipmunk had done. When everything was arranged

just right, Grandpa put the coyote box on the side of the big tree not far from the white birdhouse.

One morning several weeks later, Grandpa happened to look up at the coyote box and what do you think he saw? Suddenly three little heads poked out of the old speaker part of the box. The chipmunk babies had arrived and were now ready to run and explore all over Grandpa's place.

"Triplets!" Grandpa exclaimed. "Now you three stay right there while I go get my camera." Sure enough, when Grandpa returned they were still there ready to pose for their picture.

What a nice surprise!

Grandpa Meets a Special Chipmunk

Near Grandpa's woodshed are six big trashcans. Three hold garbage, and one is full of extra flowerpots for Grandma's potted plants. But what do you suppose is inside the other two cans? Many of the chipmunks and birds around Grandpa's place know. Can you guess?

Here is Grandpa's secret. Each month he buys 100 pounds of birdseed and 100 pounds of cracked corn. He fills the left-hand can with the birdseed and into the right-hand one goes the cracked corn.

Each morning and afternoon, Grandpa opens up the left-hand can and fills a plastic carton with the nice birdseed. Next he lifts the lid on the right-hand can and fills another carton with cracked corn.

Then he pours both cartons together into a bucket so the grain is all mixed together to feed the many birds that come to his place. Of course, the chipmunks come running for the grain too. They poke their heads out of the woodpile, run along the ground, scamper along the fence to the bird feeders and begin filling their cheek pouches. So the birds and chipmunks know all about Grandpa's secret.

One morning just as Grandpa lifted the lid to scoop up some birdseed, a chipmunk leaped from another trash can right on top of the seed and ran right up to Grandpa's hand.

"Now aren't you a friendly one?" Grandpa couldn't help smiling.

Then Grandpa noticed something. This bold chipmunk began sorting through the birdseed and choosing only the sunflower seeds. As fast as its little paws could work, it began stuffing the sunflower seeds into its cheek pouches.

Grandpa laughed. "You look just like you've got the mumps!"

Once both the cheek pouches were filled, the chipmunk turned around and jumped out of the trash can. He jumped over the top of another can, ran along the fence, and headed toward the woods to hide the nice treats.

The very next morning just as Grandpa lifted the lid to get some birdseed, the same thing happened. Then this friendly chipmunk figured out that Grandpa came in the afternoon too. It didn't take long before a regular routine started. Each time Grandpa showed up, his new little friend was right there to eat out of his hand. Grandpa liked the feel of the soft nose and tiny paws touching his hand. Each day the friendship grew stronger and stronger.

"But what shall I call you?" asked Grandpa.

The chipmunk didn't answer, but those bright little eyes kept looking up at Grandpa while he spoke.

Grandpa kept thinking and thinking of a name for his new friend. Then one morning just as he opened the back door, he heard a sharp, *"Chip! Chip! Chip!"* There right on top of the woodpile across the driveway sat his new friend calling for him. At least Grandpa was sure it was his new friend because the chipmunk didn't even budge when he quickly walked toward it. Since the woodpile was about chest high, Grandpa could easily lean over and be right close to the chipmunk's face.

"I think I'll call you Chipper," Grandpa said with a smile. "That'll suit you just fine."

"Chip! Chip! Chip!" answered Chipper.

It seemed as if Chipper had somehow told all of the relatives and friends that Grandpa really wouldn't hurt them. Soon whenever Grandpa was anywhere near the woodshed, the chipmunks began scampering around, running right across his toes, behind his heels, between his legs; chasing each other as if playing tag.

"Chipmunks, chipmunks, everywhere!" exclaimed Grandpa. "And how much fun it is to watch them!"

None of the other chipmunks seemed as friendly as Chipper though. Some quickly darted into the stack of wood and poked their heads out at Grandpa, but if he came too close, they ducked for cover and disappeared into the woodpile.

"Besides being extra tame, I wonder just how I can tell Chipper from all of the other chipmunks around here?" Grandpa thought. Then one day he got his answer. As he happened to be bending very close to Chipper's face, he noticed a tiny patch of light-colored fur on each cheek.

"Hmm," Grandpa said to himself. "That's interesting." Then speaking directly to Chipper he said, "You have special little markings. Now I can tell you apart from your friends and relatives."

Before long, Chipper began watching for Grandpa. The moment the backdoor opened, Chipper automatically began scampering across the driveway and running right up to touch the toe of Grandpa's shoe. It always made Grandpa smile.

"OK, Chipper, now you follow me and we'll go get some of those nice sunflower seeds you like so much."

But Chipper never minded Grandpa. Instead of following him like some puppy dog,

Chipper ran really fast ahead of Grandpa right across the driveway and waited for him at the chopping block.

Before long, Chipper began shelling the sunflower seeds right in front of Grandpa. Chipper's sharp little teeth easily tore open the sunflower seed and left the black shell on the chopping block. It always happened fast and was so much fun to watch.

Since Chipper liked the sunflower seeds more than anything else, Grandpa began buying a bag of these to keep on hand. Now Chipper didn't have to sort through the other seeds to get his favorites.

One morning just as Grandpa reached for a handful of sunflower seeds, he looked down and saw Chipper acting very strangely. The chipmunk was standing completely still, like it was frozen. There was no tail jerking up and down now. Chipper's head didn't turn and its paws stayed still as if its whole body had turned to stone.

"What's the matter, Chipper?" Grandpa asked. "What are you staring at?"

Then slowly Grandpa turned his head and looked up at the sky. What do you think he saw? There, soaring not far from the tops of the big spruce trees was a red-tailed hawk!

"Oh, Chipper!" Grandpa exclaimed, "you'd better run and hide!"

Just as the hawk sailed behind the tallest spruce, Chipper minded Grandpa and ran for cover deep inside the woodpile. Grandpa was glad for the safety of his stack of wood for all the chipmunks because every once in a while a big hawk came swooping overhead.

"I don't want any of my chipmunks to get caught, especially my friend, Chipper," Grandpa said to himself. "Of all God's creatures, they are about the cutest, I think."

After some time, Grandpa began adding the word "girl" to Chipper's name. He really didn't know if Chipper was a boy or girl, but since he and Grandma had two daughters, he liked the idea of adding "girl" to Chipper's name.

"Chipper girl is my special friend," he told Grandma many times.

And Grandma always nodded her head and smiled. "Yes, I know!" she said.

Whistling for the Gray Jays

Many people own pet birds. Their owners often lean close to the cage and talk to them as if they were real people. Many people open the cage and allow their bird to eat out of their hands. But have you ever wished you could be out in nature and have a wild bird fly down out of the sky and eat out of your hand or come when you called? That would be fun and exciting! Well, if you were around Grandpa's place, you would be able to see the friendliest birds in all nature. They are called Gray Jays because of their gray color. When Grandpa whistles for them, they come flying to eat some bread out of his hand or to hop close to his feet.

Many years ago when Grandpa was a young teacher, he learned firsthand about these very friendly birds and why they carry the nickname of "Camp Robber." It happened when he and some of the older schoolboys were hiking in the high country of the Olympic Mountains. They had just sat down on an old log for lunch when suddenly the Gray Jays showed up to help eat their sandwiches. Everyone liked to have these "Camp Robbers" sit on their hand and peck at their sandwiches. One boy tilted his head back and put pieces of bread on his cheek so a Gray Jay could sit on top of his head and lean over to eat. Everyone laughed and laughed. Nobody minded sharing their lunch with the bold birds.

Today Grandpa doesn't have to hike way up in the high country or go to the northern woods to see the Gray Jays. They live all around his place. This is as far south as the Gray Jays go in California and that makes Grandpa very happy.

At first, Grandpa hurried outside whenever he saw the Gray Jays all sitting on the west side fence waiting to be fed. Since Gray Jays don't eat grain like other birds, he took pieces of bread outside to feed his friends. They would all hop closer and then lean over with their mouths open to let Grandpa

feed them. This happened every day for some time.

Then one morning as he was coming around the corner of his house, a Gray Jay left the fence and flew in a nice long glide to land right on Grandpa's hand. Reaching over, it began tearing off pieces of the bread.

"Well! Well!" Grandpa exclaimed. "I guess I don't need to walk over to feed you from now on. You certainly fly faster than I can walk!"

The Gray Jay cocked its head slightly and looked at Grandpa as if to say, "That's right!"

From then on, Grandpa never fed the Gray Jays at the fence. He would break off pieces of bread and let them fly to his hand. He liked it when a Gray Jay would light on his thumb and reach over to fill its bill with the pieces of bread in the palm of his hand. But sometimes one would fly down and light on the tip of his fingers. Its sharp little claws would pinch! Whenever that happened,

Grandpa always reminded the Gray Jay of his feelings.

"Hey! That hurts! You don't need to dig in so much. My fingers are not some branch!"

Grandpa noticed that the Gray Jays often gave a little "thank you" chirp after filling their bills. It sounds something like a soft *"wheeeoooo."* Grandpa began imitating the sound with a high and low note whistle. Now whenever Grandpa wants to call his Gray Jay friends, he goes outside and makes that special whistle. If the Gray Jays are anywhere around, they will fly down from the trees and come to him. Sometimes that whistle also alerts the bright blue Steller's Jays too and they come. But Steller's Jays are scared of people and won't come real close. But they always make a lot of noise and scowl because they know the Gray Jays are not afraid.

Whenever Grandpa and Grandma go for their daily walk, Grandpa takes along about six slices of bread in plastic bags. He knows that somewhere along the usual two-mile walk there will be several groups of Gray Jays. Sometimes he whistles for them, but most of the time they spot him first and come flying in their typical flap and glide fashion even before he has a chance to whistle. They all know that somewhere in his jacket pockets are nice pieces of bread for their breakfast. If Grandpa runs out of bread while the Gray Jays are all around him, he tells them, "Come on down to the house. I've got plenty of bread there."

When a schoolteacher heard that Grandpa could feed the Gray Jays out of his hand, she brought her whole class of boys and girls over to see for themselves. But Grandpa had a surprise for them. He broke off pieces of bread and put it into their own hands.

"Now each of you hold you hands out and be real still," he told them. "I'll whistle for them, but you mustn't make a move or you might scare the birds."

Of course all of the boys and girls were excited as the Gray Jays flew down to eat out of their hands. But one little boy with a big smile rested his knee on the ground and seemed to be frozen in place like some statue. One by one the birds came to him until he ran out of bread. Then he got up and hurried to Grandpa for more bread. Just as quickly, he hurried back to his same spot and took the same position on one knee.

Children are not the only ones who have fed the Gray Jays. One winter day a group of men from the big city visited Grandpa's place. They came to count birds but especially the Gray Jays.

"We understand that you have Gray Jays around here," the leader said.

"Oh, sure," replied Grandpa. "You don't need to look around in the trees. I'll call them for you, but wait until I get some bread."

Grandpa went to the back porch where he keeps the bird bread and passed out slices to the bird-counting visitors. He told them how to break the slices up into pieces and hold out their hands. Then Grandpa lifted his head and whistled as loudly as he could. This time the Gray Jays weren't very far away and they came flying and gliding toward him immediately.

Then the funniest thing happened. One older man held out his hand and as soon as a Gray Jay came to eat, he began giggling like a little child. It was so funny to hear him and watch his happy face.

"I've never had a bird on my hand before!" he exclaimed.

Grandpa smiled. "Well, if you lived around here, you'd be able to feed the Gray Jays all the time."

Just then another man stepped forward. "I know all about Gray Jays and how bold they are. I was sitting down at a picnic table in Canada once and suddenly one of those 'Camp Robbers' flew down and snatched my whole sandwich away from me."

"Oh, they'll do that!" Grandpa agreed with a chuckle. "That's the reason I break off pieces of bread or they'd take the whole slice if I let them. Sometimes I let one of them sit on my hand and tear off chunks. They seem to like to do that."

Even when Grandpa does break off pieces for the birds, they often try to get more in their bill than they can hold. When a piece drops, they try to pick it up. But then another piece drops! "Oh! Don't get piggy-pig now!" Grandpa will warn them. "You've already got your mouth stuffed with more bread than you can hold."

Once in a while, a Gray Jay will get confused and start pecking on Grandpa's thumb as if this was food too. "Hey!" Grandpa will say, "that's my thumb! It's not something to eat!"

Gray Jays also like table scraps. "People's food," Grandpa calls it. One day he found several pieces of old pumpkin pie still in the refrigerator. Grandma suggested he feed this to his friends rather than save it any longer. No sooner had Grandpa placed the pie plate on the woodpile then the Gray Jays flew down to eat their dessert!

If the Gray Jays are really hungry, they won't wait for Grandpa's whistle. They fly down to the house looking for a handout. Sitting on top of the roof and peering over or peeking in the back porch window, they come to beg for food. Grandpa has fed them on the fence, on the deck railing, and on the big stump by the east driveway, but most of the time he puts bread on the windowsill.

He likes to put pieces of bread on his big office windowsill, too, because the Gray Jays that happen to be flying around the north side of the house can easily spot their food. The Gray Jays know exactly where they can find Grandpa most of the time. If he has forgotten to leave enough bread, they fly to the big office windowsill and look right at him as if to say, "Don't you know we're hungry? Bring some bread right away! OK?" And, of course, Grandpa stops whatever he is doing and hurries outside with some bread for his friends. Then he goes inside and watches them line up to get their meal while he finishes his office work.

Since Gray Jays nest very early in the spring, Grandpa knows he will miss seeing his friends for several months. Not until the babies are nearly fully-grown will they show up again. Grandpa has never been able to find a Gray Jay nest anywhere in the woods, but later as summer rolls around, suddenly Mama and Papa Gray Jay will bring their young down to introduce them to Grandpa. Even though they may not be tiny babies anymore, Grandpa still likes to call them "babies."

Usually he announces to Grandma, "The Gray Jay babies have arrived!"

The young Gray Jays can easily be recognized by their all slate-gray color. The young don't get their two-toned coloring until fall.

These Gray Jay youngsters are usually very cautious at first. They are a little afraid of flying right to Grandpa's hand. Instead they will fly down to wait for bread at his feet. Some have even made the mistake of lighting on top of his head! But Grandpa knows they will learn all about feeding very soon. He also knows the older ones will teach the young that as soon as they hear Grandpa whistling, it is time to wing their way toward him.

More Fun With Feathered Friends

Just as soon as Grandpa starts down the driveway with a bucket of grain, the bright blue Steller's Jays call out a noisy, *"Shaaack! Shaaack! Shaaack!"* Their loud call tells all the other birds that it is time to eat. The bigger birds come flying, the quail come running on their strong legs, and the smaller birds hiding in the bushes come flitting or hopping to be fed.

"The Steller's Jays are my announcers," Grandpa says.

It is funny to hear these announcers, but just as funny to watch them. Each time they make their loud *"Shaaack! Shaaack! Shaaack!"* their darker blue topknot goes up and down keeping time with their call.

Grandpa has learned that the Steller's Jays are great mimics too. They can imitate many other birds. In a moment they can change their voice to go *"Queeek! Queeek! Queek!"* to a soft *"Cheeep! Cheeep! Cheeep!"* Sometimes they even sound like the scream of a hawk to scare the other birds.

Whatever sounds the Steller's Jays make, Grandpa usually looks at them and smiles. "Now what are you saying?" he asks.

The only time these announcers and mimics are quiet is during nesting time in the spring. Suddenly the Steller's Jays are very still because they don't want anyone to know where they are going to raise their babies.

Of course the Steller's Jays can't imitate every bird around Grandpa's place. That is why

Grandpa loves to hear the other birds talking and chattering among themselves whenever he comes outside to feed them. Deep down in the bushes the California quail start making a soft, *"Pup! Pup! Pup!"* sound as they edge closer to the west side driveway where Grandpa has scattered the grain. They hurry along eating as they go but soon stop their talking. If they fly up to the bird feeders, they keep quiet, but they scratch around on the feeder even if they don't need to.

The daddy quail often sits atop a fencepost as a guard. If danger comes, he calls out a warning, "Be careful! Be careful!" Grandpa thinks the daddy quail's call sounds more like "Chicago! Chicago!" But whatever the call, it is a warning for all the other quail to run for cover and hide in the bushes.

During the summer, both Grandma and Grandpa love to watch the quail bring their brood of babies out of the bushes to eat. These tiny balls of light and dark brown stripes have short little legs, but they can easily keep up with their parents.

"Just look at those little buttons scurry!" Grandpa often exclaims. "They are so cute!

I think they're the cutest of all the baby birds."

Just like all mama birds, the mother quail hover over their young and protect them. But one of the most interesting things Grandpa has seen is when the daddy quail spreads his wings and squats so the babies can hurry to hide under his body too.

One of the most secretive birds around Grandpa's place is the tiny brown wrentit with its turned-up tail. This little bird only lives in the far west United States from Baja, California to the Columbia River. Since the wrentit loves to stay hidden deep in the bushes and does not like to fly across open spaces, that wide river would certainly be too far to cross.

Few people ever get to see this small bird, but Grandpa often has them hop near his feet when it is time to eat. But before he ever sees the wrentit, Grandpa can hear a soft *"Churrrr, Churrrr, Churrrr"* in the bushes. It sounds something like a small motor.

One morning right after Grandpa thought he was finished feeding all of the birds, Grandma came inside the house to tell him something. She had just returned from the cellar and had heard the little "motor" in the bushes.

"Sounds like your little bird friend is calling for you," she said.

Instead of getting more grain, Grandpa hurried outside with a slice of bread. Sure enough, just as he got near the bushes he heard the familiar *"Churrrr! Churrrr!* Breaking off a small piece of bread, he put it in his hand and knelt down close to the bushes. Slowly he slid his hand closer to the bushes. Suddenly it happened! The little wrentit hopped on his thumb, leaned over and pecked at the piece of bread. Then, just as quickly, the tiny bird disappeared into the bushes again, but Grandpa enjoyed that quick meeting so much. Wouldn't you?

Grandpa loves to hear all of the bird sounds, but he always stops and listens carefully whenever a little sparrow sings. Often, not far from Grandpa as he stands very still, the small bird will tilt its head back and sing a series of sweet notes then close with a long trill.

Grandpa always smiles. "That was such a nice song. Would you sing it again for me?"

And the sparrow will almost always sing it over again. Sometimes Grandpa will encourage the sparrow by kissing the back of his own hand. The smacking sound seems to urge the sparrow to try again, and that is just what Grandpa likes so much.

Whenever any of the birds drop some feathers on the ground, Grandpa likes to save the biggest and brightest to send to his grandchildren. But it is the downy-soft ones he likes that he saves for a special fun time in the spring.

When the swallows return to build their nests, Grandpa takes these nice, soft, fluffy feathers out of the envelope where he keeps them and goes outside. Taking one of the feathers in his hand, he holds it high and then blows on it. If the wind is just right, the little feather will float high in the air. Then suddenly a swallow will swoop down out of the sky and catch the feather in its bill and fly away to line its new nest. If the

swallow happens to miss the feather in flight, it will swing around quickly and try again.

Swallows are such swift flyers and able to twist and turn so quickly in the air, they always give Grandpa quite an air show. If the wind suddenly changes and the feather drops to the ground before any swallow can get it, Grandpa climbs up on a stump and tries again. He just wants to keep the air show going as long as the swallows are interested in catching the feathers.

If Grandpa doesn't have enough feathers, he uses little pieces of cotton. All of the swallows love the cotton too. But most of all the baby birds that will be hatched love to rest on the soft lining inside their nest.

One bird that seems to love cotton the most is the beautiful orange and black Bullock's oriole. Instead of throwing little pieces of cotton into the air, Grandpa tears off small rolls to place on the fence or on top of the fenceposts. The orioles spot the white fluff easily and come to pull chunks of the cotton off with their bills. Then they fly away to line the inside of their nests. Since their nests are like deep hanging pouches, the cotton inside makes it very soft and cozy for their babies when they hatch.

Nesting time is not the only season for fun around Grandpa's place. All year long Grandpa enjoys his feathered friends, even those bigger birds that don't come very close.

Sometimes when Grandpa is outside, a dark shadow suddenly will cross his path. Immediately he looks up into the sky because that shadow is the signal a great big turkey vulture is soaring overhead. Grandpa loves to watch these big birds with their six-foot wingspan catch the air currents and soar around and around all over the countryside. Since turkey vultures seldom flap their broad wings, they remind Grandpa of a black, feathered glider. Sometimes they fly in groups, and then the sky is filled with these black "gliders."

Grandpa considers the turkey vulture as part of nature's clean-up crew. With no feathers on their heads, they can easily eat any carcass lying around ready to rot without getting their heads messy.

Turkey vultures are so funny to watch before the sun is warm enough to heat the air so they can soar. They will perch atop the fence posts in the valley and with their huge wings spread out to dry, they slowly turn their bodies toward the sun. They do this in unison as if they are all connected together. When the air is warm enough, they give a few flaps with their big wings then up, up, and away they are airborne lifting skyward to begin the day soaring. While the hawks and eagles soar, too, Grandpa thinks the turkey vultures around his place are the best of the big soaring birds.

About a mile from Grandpa's place, the broad Pacific Ocean stretches as far as the eye can see. During the fall and winter storms, big breakers crash high along the shore sending white waves and foam as high as a house. It is exciting to watch. During those stormy times, the sound of the surf is so loud it seems as if the ocean is pounding right against the west side of the driveway.

Something else is happening during those storms. The streams overflow from the heavy rains and soon a large lake begins to form right behind the sand dunes and covers the pastureland. Since Grandpa lives right on the Pacific Flyway, the shallow lake attracts hundreds and hundreds of migrating waterfowl. Here they can spend the winter feeding and paddling around to their heart's content. Of course all of the birds are fun to watch and listen to, but the most fun are the great white tundra swans that fly all the way down from the arctic.

On bright sunny days after the rains stop, the lake is calm, reflecting the sand dunes like some giant mirror. It is even more beautiful when there are hundreds and hundreds of swans enjoying the lake! These big white

birds are three to four feet long and with about a seven-foot wingspan. With their heads held high, they swim around like kings and queens.

While some of the swans go ashore to eat the green pasture grass, their favorite way to eat is to duck their heads and necks under the water to eat the grass on the bottom of the shallow lake. Of course they look funny doing this because it seems as if they are headless, but they all seem to enjoy the underwater eating.

Whenever the swans come to the lake, Grandpa can count on many other kinds of water birds joining them. The swans don't seem to mind at all. The ducks go *"Quack, Quack"* and the geese *"Honk, Honk!"* but mixed with all this is the special musical voice of the swans chattering and talking among themselves. It all sounds like one big happy family from Grandpa's place.

Since people can't understand the swan's language, it is a great mystery just how they decide which way they will swim or fly. Sometimes a little group will break off from the rest and swim in another location on the lake or suddenly decide to lift off and fly to a flooded field in another part of the valley. Then later another group will join that one and still another until sometimes the whole lake will empty for a while. Sometimes only a pair of swans will stay on the lake all alone. Since swans mate for life, they must talk to each other in swan language as they make decisions where to go. But what are they saying among themselves? And who is making the final decision? It is a deep secret the swans have never shared, but it is all very interesting to watch.

Watching them fly with their heads sticking straight out while they sing their flying song is always so exciting to see and hear. Whether they take off in a big bunch or form a giant "V" in the sky, they always sing along to each other as they travel.

While these big swans are always enjoy-
able, the tiny hummingbirds that come to
Grandpa's place are fun to watch too. From
the dining room table, Grandpa and

Grandma can easily watch these "hummers" feeding in the flowers and sipping sugar syrup from the two feeders hanging above the deck.

Both the Anna and Allen hummingbirds buzz and zip around Grandpa's place like so many natural little helicopters. It is easy to tell them apart. The male Anna has a rose-red head and throat that flashes different shades in the sunlight. His greenish wings and body fairly sparkle. The little female has green wings and body with a red throat-patch. But both the male and female Allen hummingbirds are like so much fire in the sky. Their reddish-orange coloring easily identifies them. And the male Allen has a fiery temper to match his coloring. Grandpa thinks it is so funny to watch this little grump. He will sit on the fence near a feeder just waiting to chase away any hummingbird that comes close. Even though he may not be hungry himself, he thinks it is HIS feeder and won't let anyone else around. Not only will he chase other hummingbirds, but bigger birds as well!

With so many varieties of birds, acting in so many different ways, it is always exciting and fun around Grandpa's place. The great big picture windows in the house make it not only easy to see the beautiful scenery, but to enjoy those fine-feathered friends as well.

Woody and His Wood Rat Relatives

Not far from Grandpa's place are several strange-looking, round stacks of dried twigs and branches about four feet wide and as high as a man's head. At first glance these stacks of dried twigs and branches reminded Grandpa of a beaver lodge, but since no beaver dam or pond was anywhere around, it could not be a beaver lodge. And besides, the rounded stacks were not built with mud.

"Who could be living inside these houses?" Grandpa wondered.

Then when he asked an old-timer who had lived in the area all his life, he learned the secret. "Those are wood rat nests," the old-timer told Grandpa. "They're clean little animals. Inside their houses are as many as seven bathrooms. The problem with wood rats, though, is the fact they like to carry things off. They even got into my storage shed and moved nuts and bolts around!"

Grandpa found out that the wood rat is really a pack rat. The early pioneers of this country named them "trade rats" because they thought these creatures were trading sticks and twigs for utensils or whatever they could find. Later it was discovered that they were not trading at all but simply moving whatever they could find.

One morning when Grandpa was feeding the birds and chipmunks, he caught a glimpse of something gray moving in the woodshed. It was too big for a chipmunk and certainly not a bird. There it was again!

It was a wood rat that had moved into his woodshed for the winter!

Grandpa right then and there decided to put out some sunflower seeds on the chopping block inside the woodshed. Sure enough, the wood rat came to get the sunflower seeds as if it expected the food. Then quickly it turned around and disappeared into the woodpile. Day after day, Grandpa would watch his new friend scoop up the sunflower seeds in its little white paws, put the grain into its mouth, then turn around and hurry back inside the woodpile to hide the nice food.

Grandpa smiled. "I'm going to call you 'Woody.' And Woody, you've certainly picked a nice place to live."

Every year Grandpa buys a big stack of pine or redwood kindling blocks. Some are nearly square, but others are thin sticks about a foot or so long. Suddenly one day he noticed some of his kindling stuffed way up near the rafters on top of the neatly stacked hardwood.

"I didn't put any kindling up there!" he exclaimed. Then he thought for a moment. "Oh! That must be Woody moving my kindling at night."

Sure enough! Woody was busy, busy, busy. He even put some kindling way out on the roof of the woodshed and would pile little stacks of kindling and other sticks on top of the chopping block sometime during the night. In order to feed him in the morning, Grandpa would have to brush the little pile aside to make room for the sunflower seeds. Then Grandpa started a habit of knocking on the side of the woodshed to let Woody know he had arrived.

"Breakfast is served, Woody! Come get your breakfast!"

And without fail Woody would poke his head out from the woodpile, sniff a little, and look around with his big buggy eyes, then climb atop the chopping block to get his breakfast of sunflower seeds.

One morning when Grandpa came out to the woodshed to call Woody, he suddenly stopped short and blinked. "Did I just see two heads?" he asked himself.

Sure enough! Out between the cracks of the neatly stacked wood came another wood rat!

Grandpa hurried back to the house to tell Grandma the news. "What shall I call this newcomer?" he asked.

"Oh, call him 'Woody Junior,'" suggested Grandma.

So inside the woodshed were Woody and Woody Junior all cozy and comfortable. They must have had all sorts of nests and sunflower seeds stored away throughout the woodpile.

One day, Grandma called Grandpa to come look at the flowerbed around the woodshed. "My iris flower is being eaten right down to the ground," she said as she pointed to the stubby looking tips of iris. "I think it's your wood rat friends, Woody and Woody Junior, are doing the damage."

"Oh, I don't think so," answered Grandpa with a frown. "It must be some other creature."

"Well, I think it's the wood rats," Grandma answered.

And Grandma was right. The wood rats were nibbling on her nice flowers outside the woodshed. Grandpa made a test to be sure. He picked some wild irises that grow in the woods and fields around his place and put some on the chopping blocks inside the woodshed. Soon all the wild iris stems were gone! Both Woody and Woody Junior wanted those fresh greens for their dinner.

Since the woodpile had been used up on both the south and west sides where the irises were growing, Grandpa put down some wire to keep his wood rat friends from eating Grandma's nice flowers. Later he found something even better to keep the wood rats from nibbling on the irises.

Since Grandma had some extra string beans from her garden, he started putting a little handful on each chopping block. Sure enough! By morning all of the string beans were gone!

When Grandpa told Grandma the news, she nodded her head. "Well, that's a lot better than eating my flowers. As it gets later in the season and the string beans get too old for us to eat, you can have plenty for your wood rats."

One morning Grandpa was surprised to find only Woody Junior coming to eat his breakfast. Woody had strangely disappeared, but Grandpa didn't need to worry about Woody Junior being alone. Not long after this, another wood rat showed up. Grandpa could tell by the size and coloring that it was not the original Woody.

"Well, well!" exclaimed Grandpa. "Now you've got a new relative living with you, Woody Junior!"

But that wasn't all. In a few days, another wood rat showed up to share the breakfast. Just as Grandpa was getting used to watching the three wood rats happily eating, a baby wood rat popped its head up from the left-hand chopping block, climbed over toward Grandpa, and started scooping up the sunflower seeds too. Grandpa's eyes opened wide.

"My, oh my! A baby too! Look at all those wood rats!"

When Grandpa told Grandma about the big family of four wood rats in the wood-shed, she shook her head. "We're getting way too many wood rats," she said. "I think you ought to trap all but one and release the rest up the road a ways."

Grandpa agreed he would do that, but first he wanted to try something. The baby wood rat looked so soft and silky, he just wanted to see if he could feel the fur once. Both Woody and Woody Junior had come up to his hands and wiggled their whiskers around his fingers, but he had never felt the back of either of them. Ordinarily Grandpa never tries to touch any of the wild animals but always lets them come to him. "Woody Baby," as he began calling the littlest one, was different. The fur looked so soft, he just couldn't resist trying to feel it.

Shortly after this, Woody Baby came right up to his hand as he was putting sunflower seeds on the chopping block. Grandpa reached over and let his fingers touch the baby's back. The little wood rat didn't seem to mind, so Grandpa stroked its back again. It was the softest fur he had ever felt.

"I think when I trap the wood rats, I'll keep Woody Baby," he told Grandma.

Grandpa had a plan. He would set his live trap near the chopping blocks and bait it with sunflower seeds. Once a wood rat was caught, he would put the trap with the rat in the trunk of his car and drive about a mile and a half up the road and let it loose.

The scheme worked fine. The very next morning one of the wood rats was caught inside the trap. He took it for a ride in the trunk of his car, and as soon as he opened the trap door, the rat scampered away into the brush.

The very next morning he caught Woody Junior and repeated the drive to same spot. But just as he started to let Woody Junior loose, he felt really sad.

"I hate to see you go, Woody Junior. You've been such a good friend."

After he drove back to the house and told Grandma how sad he felt, she looked at Grandpa and said, "Maybe you should have saved Woody Junior and let all the others go." Then she paused and shook her head. "But it's too late now."

To Grandpa's surprise, the next morning he caught two in the same trap, Woody Baby and one of the relatives. He took both up to the same spot where the others had been turned loose, but when he opened the trap door, he had to keep his hand in front of the opening or Woody Baby would get out too. The other wood rat turned back as if waiting for Woody Baby but finally hurried on to join the others.

After Grandpa took Woody Baby back to the woodshed, he noticed that it didn't come when he called. Being trapped had scared Woody Baby, but in a few days, he showed up again.

Not only did Woody Baby show up, but guess what happened? Surprise! Surprise! Another wood rat showed up alongside Woody Baby. This one had a little more brown color, so Grandpa named him "Woody Browny."

For a long time, Grandpa had wanted to see at least one of his wood rat friends take the green beans he put on the chopping blocks, but the greens were always taken at night when he was asleep. Then one morning he decided to put a little pile of string beans on a chopping block and just wait to see how a wood rat moved them. In a few minutes Woody Browny showed up. He sniffed the green beans, took one in his mouth crosswise and started to go into a small wood tunnel in the big stack of wood. Suddenly Woody Browny stopped. The string bean was caught crosswise. What did he do? He turned the string bean sideways and quickly moved it through the tunnel.

Grandpa thought that he probably would never again be surprised at what he discovered in the woodshed. But he was wrong! As Woody Baby grew up to a full-size wood rat, he noticed something. Woody Baby had a big tummy!

"I was wrong about Woody Baby," he told Grandma. "It's not a boy after all and she looks very pregnant to me."

Sure enough! Not long after this Grandpa saw two tiny wood rats about the size of field mice scampering around the bottom of the chopping blocks.

When he came back into the house, he told Grandma what he had just seen. "Now we have at least four wood rats again!" he said with a big smile.

"Oh, my!" Grandma said as she smiled back. Then she shook her head a little. "It looks like this will be an ongoing thing."

Grandpa agreed. The woodshed would always have plenty of wood rats.

And All the Other Animals

On the north side of the woodshed, six steps down to a lower level, is the cellar. Here it stays cool all year long. This is a great place to store fresh fruit and vegetables. On the shelves are jars and jars of canned tomatoes, peaches, and applesauce which Grandma cans each year. Also there are boxes and boxes of fresh apples which Grandpa and Grandma pick every fall so they can have apples to eat all during the winter and spring. Whenever any of the apples start to spoil, Grandpa goes down to the cellar and cuts out the rotten part and throws it away. Can you guess what he does with the rest of the apple? No, he doesn't eat it himself, nor does Grandma. He feeds it to the deer that just love apples!

It wasn't long before the deer figured out that Grandpa stored those juicy apples in the cellar. Sometimes while he walks down to the cellar, they wait nearby for him to toss them the fresh fruit. Often when they are near the cellar, Grandpa calls to them because they move away when he comes too close.

"If you'll just wait a little, I'll get you some apples."

The deer are a little afraid of all humans and keep their distance, but they stop and look right at Grandpa with their ears forward and their eyes sharply focused right on him. Ordinarily they would run away, but they know that he is going to get them something special to eat. After Grandpa cuts out the rotten spots and throws them away, he walks a little way from the cellar and tosses pieces of the good part not far from his of-fice window. That way when he goes inside, he can easily watch the deer enjoy their breakfast without disturbing them.

One morning Grandpa didn't see any deer at all. "They must still be back in the woods," he said to himself.

As usual, he went to the cellar to sort through the apples to cut up a few pieces of the good parts to feed the deer. Just as he was leaving the cellar with his hands full, he stopped short. There right in front of the

doorway were two little heads peeking around the corner at him.

"Oh, my!" he exclaimed. "Twin fawns!"

And right behind these two spotted youngsters stood their mother. All three were waiting for their breakfast of apples. They quickly moved back a little when he stepped forward to toss the pieces of apples. As the three were eating, Grandpa hurried back to the house to tell Grandma.

Just as he entered the kitchen, Grandma was waiting for him with a big smile. "It was so cute!" she exclaimed. "As you headed down to the cellar, those twins and the doe came trotting along the west side driveway to catch up with you."

"I wish I could have seen that, but you should have seen those little heads peeking around the corner at me," Grandpa answered.

It is so much fun to watch the deer, but Grandpa and Grandma had a big problem. Besides apples, the deer love roses and many different flowers, too. That's why it was necessary to fence in the front yard. Grandma has such a beautiful flower garden there. Now the deer can look, but they can't eat her roses and lovely flowers.

One day while Grandpa was looking out his office window, he saw something walking through the tall grass right toward the place where he puts out the pieces of apple. It was a nice big gray fox with a long bushy tail!

"Well, what do you know!" Grandpa exclaimed, "Mr. Fox likes apples too!"

Right then and there Grandpa decided he had better put out some apples on the chopping block near the garbage cans because the deer might not like to share their apples with the fox. In no time at all, the fox learned about the new place. "Foxie," as Grandpa called him, would wait in the bushes nearby and then slip quietly up to the chopping block to get his fresh pieces of apple. Not many days later, however, Grandpa felt uncomfortable about all this.

"I'm worried about feeding Foxie on the chopping block," he told Grandma. "That's the same spot where the chipmunks feed and not far away are the wood rats."

What should he do? Then an idea came to him. The giant eucalyptus tree close to the fence on the east side driveway was already scheduled to be cut down. It was growing much too close to the power line, and if it fell down during a windstorm, it could cause all sorts of damage. Already some limbs had broken off so Grandpa planned to have it cut down.

"And I could use the big stump for a feeding station," he told Grandma. "But I wonder how long it would take Foxie to find the new spot?"

"Oh, don't worry," Grandma said, "he'll find it very soon."

And she was right. The very next day after the tree was cut, Foxie leaped up on the stump and started eating the pieces of apple. It was then that Grandpa and Grandma noticed a little fox habit. Instead of eating all the time, the fox would jerk its head up ever so often and with pointed ears look down the driveway to see if anything was coming.

Grandpa decided that pieces of apple were not enough food for the fox, so he began putting out table scraps and buying dog food. Next to the bowl full of dog food, Grandpa began putting out two dog biscuits as an extra treat. Every evening about sundown Foxie would faithfully come for his meal. Sometimes he would come earlier, but Grandpa and Grandma could always count on his coming.

Then one afternoon, guess what happened? It was a real surprise. Two foxes showed up at once!

"Come here and look at this!" Grandpa called to Grandma. "Now we have Mr. and Mrs. Fox! It won't be just Foxie anymore."

From inside the back porch, Grandpa and Grandma could easily watch through the windows without scaring them. Without snarling or fighting over the food, the two ate side by side as they shared their meal. Sometimes one would

lift its head to check down the driveway, but there was never any quarreling over the meal.

Grandpa soon learned that the gray fox loved other fruit besides apples. Whenever there were some extra grapes that he and Grandma didn't want to eat, he would put them out on the stump. The foxes would always gobble the grapes down as if they were some dessert.

"Notice how Mr. and Mrs. Fox eat so daintily," he said. It was true. Instead of gobbling their food and being sloppy, the fox always chews and nibbles very nicely. It was so much fun to watch them!

One evening just about the time when Mr. and Mrs. Fox usually come to eat, someone else was already on the stump.

"Look at that!" Grandpa cried. "Come quick and see this!"

Grandma hurried to the back porch. There munching on the dog food was a great big raccoon! She took one look and smiled. "Well, I guess it's first come first served from now on. Mr. and Mrs. Fox had better get here earlier if they want something to eat."

Grandpa had seen a short-tailed raccoon eating leftover birdseed on the bird feeder one evening. He immediately called him "Stubbytail" and was amazed at how he could climb up a steel pipe pole that held the bird feeder. When he was through eating, he would grasp the pipe with his front paws while his back paws slid down the pipe like a fireman going down a fire pole.

But this was not Stubbytail. When Grandpa turned on the back porch flood light for a better view, Mr. Raccoon simply looked up for a few seconds and then went right back to munching on the free meal. With a dark band across their eyes, raccoons look like some furry bandit. Not only do they look like a bandit, but they also often act like one. Before an electric wire was fixed on top of the high deer fence around the garden, the raccoons were climbing over and stealing the nice corn at night.

It didn't take long for Mr. and Mrs. Fox to figure out that they had better start coming earlier if they wanted to get their meal. Once Grandpa actually saw all three out there by the stump at once. The raccoon was right next to one fox while the other fox had just jumped down and was trotting away. A few nights later came a

greater surprise. Who should be on the stump before anyone else showed up but a great big opossum!

"Come quick!" Grandpa called to Grandma. "I've never seen such a big opossum in my life!"

Mr. Opossum seemed to feel that he belonged there and was helping himself to all the food. As Grandma had said, "It's first come, first served from now on!"

Since many people know that Grandpa feeds so many birds, a friend of his gave him a most interesting gift one day. It was called a "Quail Block." This big solid brown block was filled with all sorts of good things that were supposed to attract the quail. Grandpa decided to build a little shed for the "Quail Block" with a floor and roof so it would not get washed away in the rain. He put it right outside his office window on the west side of the driveway so he could watch the quail come peck on this chunk of special food. But who do you think came to eat? No, it was not the quail! Nor did the birds seem interested. Rabbits came out of the bushes and soon found out that the "Quail Block," filled with nice sweet molasses and grain was really good eating. "Yum Yummy!" they must have thought.

"I think I'll call it the 'Bunny Block' instead," Grandpa chuckled.

Grandma agreed, but she shook her head. "But we don't want any more bunnies around here."

That was true. Rabbits love flowers! Even though the front yard is all fenced in, Grandma has nice bright flowers growing along the driveway. Both Grandpa and Grandma agreed that little "Hop Hops" as they liked to call them, just had to be caught in the live trap and taken up the road to find a new home. Year after year, Grandpa had been doing this anyway.

"But now with the 'Bunny Block' drawing them here, I'll have to start setting the trap again," Grandpa said.

That was when something happened that he hadn't counted on. A neighbor came by and told Grandpa he had caught something besides a rabbit.

"Do you know you've caught a civet cat?" the neighbor asked.

What the neighbor meant was that Grandpa had captured a little spotted skunk. These are not as large as the striped skunks, but they can perfume the air with a big stink.

"Oh, no!" Grandpa exclaimed. "I'll have to be very careful when I release the trap. What'll I do?"

Then he had an idea. He put on his raincoat and pants and gloves just in case the spotted skunk let go with a stinking spray. That way he could wash off outside without getting his clothes all smelly.

When he came to the trap he was so surprised. The spotted skunk had obviously been very busy while Grandpa was changing into his rain gear. It hadn't been bumping its head against the opening or fighting the cage like other animals might do. Instead, it had reached its little paws through the wire mesh and grabbed lots of dried grass and weeds to make a cozy little nest in the corner of the trap and had gone sound to sleep. When Grandpa opened the trap door, the spotted skunk poked its head out from the cozy nest, blinked its eyes, and slowly walked away without even raising its tail as a warning that it might spray.

Not long after this, Grandpa caught another spotted skunk and it, too, did the same thing. It was a real lesson for Grandpa.

"Now I know what to do if I find myself in a stressful situation," he said. "Just calm down and take a nap!"

Of course baiting the trap with cracked corn kept Grandpa busy catching rabbits. Then one morning when he went outside to check the trap, he found a baby raccoon inside. Instead of being quiet like the spotted skunks, it was snarling and acting really angry. That was why Grandpa was very careful when he let it loose right in the yard. He didn't want to get bitten!

Besides protecting the flowers outside the fence, the redwood trees Grandpa planted had to be protected too. Some bark had been torn off one of the trees and that signaled something. Can you guess what animal likes to eat bark? It is none other than Mr. Porcupine.

One night after Grandpa turned on the back porch light, he saw a big, fat porcupine headed down the driveway toward the redwood trees. The live trap was much too small to catch this big porcupine. Grandpa had an idea. He hurried over and grabbed an empty garbage can and got a shovel. He wasn't going to try and scoop up the porcupine, but after turning the garbage can on its side, he gently guided the porcupine toward the garbage can with the shovel. He didn't want to hurt Mr. Porcupine nor did he want any of those sharp needles stuck in his legs either. Once inside the garbage can, Grandpa turned it right side up, put the lid on it, picked the whole thing up, and carried it to the garage with Mr. Porcupine inside. Opening the trunk to his car, he picked up the garbage can and put it inside the trunk and left the trunk lid open.

"I'm going to take Porky for a ride," he told Grandma.

Then driving down the road about five miles, he found a nice brushy spot. Grandpa stopped the car and went back to the trunk. After lifting the garbage can onto the road, he took off the lid and carefully turned the garbage can on its side.

"OK, Porky, you're free now," Grandpa said.

Mr. Porcupine staggered out and stopped for air.

"Oh, I'm sorry," apologized Grandpa. "I forgot to leave a little air space for you. But you'll be all right."

Mr. Porcupine slowly waddled off into the bushes and Grandpa never saw him again.

Not everything that creeps, crawls, hops, waddles, or walks has been seen around Grandpa's place. Sometimes the howling and yapping of coyotes can be heard at night, but neither Grandpa nor Grandma have seen any coyotes even though they have even heard them as close as up by the garden.

The funniest sound, however, is the voice of a little tree frog happily croaking near the sliding glass door in the dining room that leads to the deck in the front yard. Nobody can find the little fellow. Other green tree frogs have often been seen hopping around in the flowerbeds, but this one seems to be living right inside the house. At least it sounds that way!

"He's our house frog," says Grandma.

Grandpa and Grandma have looked and looked but have never been able to find him. One day two visitors were determined to find him when he kept croaking so loudly, but they, too, finally had to give up. He is a real ventriloquist. Sometimes his croaking sounds like it might be down by the sliding glass door trough or just outside on the glass itself, and then again up in the potted plant hanging near the door. It is a great mystery where he might be. But wherever he is and however loudly he croaks, it is just one more thing that makes life all the more interesting around Grandpa's place.

If you enjoyed this book, you'll enjoy these other books:

Nibbles the Mostly Mischievous Monkey

Martha Myers. Jean's pet squirrel monkey loves pranks and seems to always be laughing. He sits on a hot stove, swallows pain pills, and turns Mitzie, the family dachshund, into a puppy taxi by hitching rides on her back. When Nibbles escapes from his cage one day, Jean and Allen learn to trust that God will take care of them in every situation.

0-8163-1947-2. Paperback.
US$6.99, Can$11.49.

Petunia, the Ugly Pug

Heather Grovet. This story about a pug with a face only a mother could love, delights while it teaches about kindness to God's precious animals, and loving acceptance of ourselves. Kids will love this sweet story about Kyla and a silly little dog named Petunia that is anything but perfect.

0-8163-1871-9. Paperback.
US$6.99, Can$11.49.

Prince, the Persnickety Pony

Heather Grovet. Janelle Wilson had been praying for a pony for years. But Prince was anything *but* charming! Will Jesus listen to her prayer about winning a ribbon at the fair and keeping Prince after the summer? Teaches kids about caring for horses and how God answers prayers.

0-8163-1787-9. Paperback.
US$6.99, Cdn$11.49.

Order from your ABC by calling **1-800-765-6955**, or get online and shop our virtual store at **www.AdventistBookCenter.com**.

- Read a chapter from your favorite book
- Order online
- Sign up for email notices on new products